Catullus

VERSIONS WITH A FOREWORD BY

PETER VALENTE

Spuyten Duyvil
New York City

I would like to thank Ed Foster who published some of these versions online at talismanmag.net. Some of them also appeared in my selection *Let the Games Begin: Five Roman Writers* (Talisman House, 2015).

©2018 Peter Valente
ISBN 978-1-947980-00-6

Library of Congress Cataloging-in-Publication Data

Names: Catullus, Gaius Valerius, author. | Valente, Peter, 1970- translator.
Title: Catullus : versions with a foreword / by Peter Valente.
Description: New York City : Spuyten Duyvil, 2018. | Includes bibliographical references.
Identifiers: LCCN 2017044281 | ISBN 9781947980006
Subjects: LCSH: Catullus, Gaius Valerius--Translations into English.
Classification: LCC PA6275.E5 V35 2018 | DDC 874/.01--dc23
LC record available at https://lccn.loc.gov/2017044281

Introduction: Catullus' Circle Of Friends

Catullus was born into a wealthy family of Verona, around 82 B.C. He was a punk rocker of the Latin world, but he had a heart of gold and was, above all, a great poet. In poem 1, he applauds Cornelius' bold effort to "explicate the history of the world in just three papyrus rolls," and offers him his book. Cornelius Nepos was an historian from Cisalpine Gaul who wrote a three-volume history, *Chronica*. Let's imagine that this is Catullus' first book of poems and that he gives it to his mentor. He did, in fact, dedicate his poems to Nepos. In the poem he is modest, but at the same time bold, asserting that the book "will be remembered for all eternity." He can be gentle with "Veranius," whom he affectionately calls "Veran," taking him into his home after his travels, and listening to his stories, desiring to "kiss your mouth, your sweet eyes." He is happy in the company of his friend. Then there's "Lesbia," the woman that scholars believe Catullus fell in love with in Rome. Her real name was Clodia, and she was the daughter of Appius Claudius Pulcher, Consul in 79 B.C., and sister of Clodius Pulcher. She belonged to a distinguished Latin family. To Catullus, she is "the epitome of beauty." But, Catullus writes in poem 86, it her very beauty "that attracts all these other women to her." During the Roman Imperial era references to same-sex relations between women are more frequent than during the Republic. Since Romans believed that the sexual act required a dominant and a passive partner and was essentially "phallic" in character, portrayals of women included phallic acts, such as penetrating boys with a dildo. In poem 79, Catullus speaks of Lesbia's desire to obtain his boy for pleasure. Clodia married Caecilius Metellus Celer, in 63 B.C. and was eventually suspected of poisoning him to death. Catullus, who had an affair with her during her marriage, speaks about her terrible rages and insults her husband by suggesting he knows this aspect of her personality very well indeed:

Lesbia screams and insults me in front of her husband
and the simple-minded fool simply grins. He's evidently content
and knows nothing! Listen now, you mule!, if she could forget about me she'd shut up
and not throw these crazy fits: but because she whines like a little girl
and hurls curses at me means she remembers me, and what is
much worse, infinitely worse, is that when she's really pissed (like now!)

she works herself up into a state of rage beyond belief
and then begins to talk and talk and talk!

After her husband's death, she has an affair with Caeluis, one of Catullus' friends. In the following poem, Catullus suffers a fit of jealousy as Lesbia ignores him and fixes her eyes on yet another man:

> To me that man over there seems equal to a god
> and I mean no offense to any sacred law,
> but I think he even surpasses the gods.
> He sits opposite you, repeatedly looks at you and listens,
> I can hear your sweet laughter ringing in my ears,
> and I am quickly silenced.
> The result is my wretched state,
> all my sense leaves me. Why?
> Because I realize as he looks at you, Lesbia,
> nothing remains for me.
>
> * * * * * * *
>
> My tongue is numb, a fire burns in my groin.
> Now my ears are ringing with the sound
> of their mutual laughter. I am insane with jealousy!
> Thankfully, the night covers both my eyes in darkness.
> Idleness, Catullus, that is your trouble,
> the reason for your manic static and paralyzing despair.
> Remember, a life of leisure has brought kings to their knees
> and prosperous cities to utter ruin.

She even lures a man that Catullus himself was interested in away from him. He is weakened and hurt by her fluctuating love and writes, "it's just the same story over and over again. / Her words can't be trusted. / They might as well have been written in the air."

On the other hand, there is the fury and hatred that Catullus expresses in the poems. Catullus will not be pushed around or, to put it more plainly, and in contemporary terms: he wouldn't have taken lightly being called a faggot in the street. In poem 16 he tells Aurelius and Furius that he'll "face-fuck and sodomize" them both if they think that because he writes lines like 'I'll give you a thousand kisses' his virility is compromised. They think his verses are indecent and "prissy." He writes, "the true poet should be chaste in his life but not necessarily in his verses." He also challenges Ravidus who thinks only a "corrupt mind" would read his verses. The Filth and the Fury all over again! Catullus makes the headlines and the caption reads: "Catullus face-fucks Ravidus to death." It should be noted here that there was a difference between Roman and Greek homosexuality. The Romans, in fact, had no precise term for homosexuality or heterosexuality. The dichotomy with regard to sexuality was expressed as active (sodomy)/masculine and passive (fellatio) / feminine. Roman men were free to have sex with males without any perceived loss of masculinity or social status, provided that they took the dominant role which meant penetration. For this reason, in poem 80, Catullus mocks Gellius whom he believes engages secretly in oral sex with men. In poem 15 he threatens Aurelius. Catullus tells him that if he has sex with his boy, Juventius, he will stuff radishes and mallets into his anus. And then there is Marcus Tullius (Cicero), who is only one in a line of pompous orators that Catullus satirizes:

49. AD MARCUM TULLIUM CICERONEM

You're one of the most eloquent orators
from the descendants of Romulus
and there are just as many others now,
Marcus Tullius,
and more to come!,
But thank you for thinking of me,
the great Catullus
the worst poet,
the absolute worst,
just like you who are the Patron of all!
p.s. I wish you my best.

Then there are the complicated relationships with Gellius and Juventius. Gellius was a consul in 36 B.C. and a commander in Mark Antony's navy at Actium in 31 B.C. He has an affair with Clodia and with his uncle's wife. He is also accused by the Senate of having an affair with own his step-mother. In poem 89, Catullus emphasizes Gellus' "thinness" as a quality of moral depravity. Catullus is implying that he is "thin" like a girl.

In the Roman world a feminine man was looked down upon and likely to be passive in a sexual encounter. His "femininity" was in opposition to the Roman "cult of virility." Catullus sums up his opinion of Gellius in poem 91, after having found out about his affair with Clodia : "you delight in every game, no matter what, / as long as it's even a tiny bit transgressive." Juventius, Catullus' boy-friend, was born into a rich family. In Roman antiquity boys were bought and sold as sex objects but the buyer needed the owner's permission before having sex with his boy. In poem 15, Catullus tells Aurelius, "When you're randy, I know you'll fuck anything! / But please keep away from my boyfriend, Juventius." Juventius consistently frustrates Catullus' love. Poem 81 is characteristic:

81. AD IUVENTIUM

Juventius, from all the pretty men in all the bathhouses in Rome,
couldn't you have picked up
someone other than this young punk
from the filthy district of Pisaurum?
The only thing yellower than his complexion
is that old gilded statue of Caesar!
And, to make matters worse,
you say he turns you on!
You mean you like him more than me?
Can't you see you're being a real asshole?

Catullus' poems are a Dionysian orgy of lust and ecstasy and hatred that clash with the genteel, aristocratic heritage, whose embodiment is the affluent Clodia, whose family was of the famous Claudian line. She rejects him and causes him great pain on numerous occasions. Even the boy, Juventius, and the young man, Gellius, are figures of deceit and prove unfaithful and resistant to Catullus' love. Finally in poem 105, Catullus writes:

Mr. Cock strives to climb up the Parnassus,
but the Muses (those sluts!) prick him with their pitchforks and yell, "GET OUT"!

Catullus' sadism is driven as much by love's failure as by a geniune disgust with pompous orators and pretension in all its forms. Clodia's own pretentiousness and profligate nature make Catullus unable to maintain friendly feelings towards her. In fact, the more he loves her the less he is able to treat her with kindness. In her presence he reverts to the figure of an innocent schoolboy trying to impress her. She is permanently on the defensive, seated on a pedestal too high for him to reach her. A moment of tenderness occurs with Caelius, with whom he develops a "unique friendship" during a time when the "furious flame scorched my genitals", perhaps when he was younger or during a moment of loneliness. He wishes him success in love and happiness. But it this same Caelius who, on another occasion, will betray Catullus with Clodia. One rare instance of real affection and love occurs with Veranius, and not with Lesbia, with whom he shares sporadic moments of happiness in an otherwise hopeless love, nor with Ipsitilla, a prostitute with whom Catullus merely has sex, nor with the vain Gellius and not, finally, with the boy, Juventius. I believe it is important to note that, despite the popularity of the many poems written to Lesbia, which are largely a catalogue of difficulties and failures, and admittedly of great lyrical power, if one is to find moments of real tenderness and love, however transitory, in Catullus' poetry, one has to look to his relations with his male friends. He is a punk with a big heart but not a *pathicus*, a poet of great lyric power and wit, but not someone to mess with when his anger is aroused.

At last there are the following fragments that could serve as an epitaph:

1.

I dedicate to you and consecrate this sacred grove, Priapus…….
in Lampsacus, where your house is and sacred grove
…….. Priapus……. especially for you,
who are worshiped at the mouth of the Hellespont, in the cities
and elsewhere.

2.

my passion is the MEAT

3.

you won't escape the bite of my poem

Here Catullus praises Priapus, a fertility god marked by a large, permanently erect penis. Fragment 3 is interesting. Perhaps he is speaking of his doomed love for Clodia, his burning anger and disgust, or does it simply express his confident attitude that his enemies in general will not escape his ridicule and fury? Much of Latin poetry has been consigned to oblivion. Let us be thankful for what remains, and above all for the poetry of Gaius Valerius Catullus.

A Note On The Translation

This selection of Catullus' poetry, which focuses on his relation to his circle of friends, is not strictly a literal translation yet attempts to capture his spirit and bring him up to date. Thus, there are occasional anachronisms, like "Doc Martins" or "Poland Spring" or "The Times" newspaper, or colloquial expressions like "health nut" or "sloshed." In many cases I also elaborate on the implications of certain lines and embellish them with my own invention, hoping to stay within bounds of what Catullus "might have said" or what the poem implies. It is my attempt to make the poems as vivid as I can. I am thinking of Derek Jarman's film "Caravaggio," which did the same thing with the story of Caravaggio's life as I am doing here. When it was presented to scholars in Italy it was uniformly applauded.

The following is one example from poem 112. The Latin is:

Multus homo es, Naso, neque tecum multus homo
    te scindat: Naso, multus es et pathicus.

In my translation:

You're a whole lot of man, Naso, and yet many men dare ram their
                                            prick into your ass:
Naso, you're one hell of a big guy and yet you take it from behind!

I choose the colloquial expression, "you're one hell of a big guy" to stand for the affectionate, "large man" (*Multus homo*). But more significant, for my translation, is the word *pathicus* which, in this case, I translate as "take it from behind." *Pathicus* is a word that refers to a passive partner, a catamite. And also, for the line that means, literally, " not many men wouldn't / split you" (*neque tecum multus homo / te scindat*) which can be translated, roughly as "to use for anal sex", I have translated, "dare ram their prick into your ass." The poem's point is that however big Naso is he is still a *pathicus*. I've developed the passage and made it more vivid with, "Naso, you're one hell of a big guy and yet you take it from behind." This is representative of my translation practice. Also, on occasion, I will put, in parenthesis, certain exclamatory statements, that I believe clarify and add to what Catullus is implying in a poem. In certain cases, this is also to amplify the humorous effects. I believe that the "wildness" of subject matter in Catullus' poems calls for such transgression of conventional translation practices.

1. A<small>D</small> C<small>ORNELIUM</small>

To whom, above all, will I give my new elegant book,
polished just now with dry pumice stone?
Why to you, Cornelius: you who always
held in high esteem my juvenile poetic efforts.
Then as now, you were courageous.
You alone among the Italians
dared to write the history of the world in just three papyrus scrolls…
By almighty Jupiter, your brilliance set the standard for scholarship!
So take this little book,
for whatever it's worth, and may it, O Muse,
be remembered for all eternity!

9. AD VERANIUM

Veran, if I had three hundred thousand friends it wouldn't matter to me at all
because you are here now, you have come back home, like you promised,
to your caring brothers and dear old mother.
You're safe and sound in this place. I can't wait to hear
your account of the wild regions of the Spanish,
of their various exploits and the nature of the different clans.
I know you enjoy telling of your adventures and I so love to hear your voice.
But, as you turn your sweet neck toward me,
will you let me kiss your mouth, your lovely eyes?
Catullus, you are the happiest man alive!

70. Ad Lesbiam

When the subject of marriage comes up
her eyes take on a peculiar glow and she looks at me
and says that I'm the only one she wants as her husband.
She says, Forget about Jove! But I wasn't born yesterday.
When a woman says this to her devoted lover,
it's just the same story over and over again.
Her words can't be trusted.
They might as well have been written in the air
or on a fast-moving current flowing out to sea.
A minute later she'll wake up from her dream
and she'll say she hates everything about me!

71. Revenge

If a person finds offensive the smell of a goat in the armpit
or anyone who is cut down by the crippling gout,
then this rival of yours, who keeps your lover busy (until she can hardly walk!)
sick himself from both, is delightfully evil in his practice
for as often as he fucks her (and the bitch likes it!) he's revenged on you both:
she smells the stench and vomits, he's ruined from the gout.

113. Where Did They Come From?

Cinna, during Pompey's first time as consul there were two men who both took turns with Maecilia. Now that he's consul again, those two men are still here, but a thousand rivals have sprouted up next to each. Semen must have been falling from the sky!
In any case, Adultery is fruitful!

79. AD LESBIUM

Lesbius is a pretty boy. So why not? After all Lesbia prefers
him to you, Catullus, and all your kind.
Yes, but let him try to sell Catullus and all his kind
if he can find three people who can confirm who his father is!

89: Ad Gellium

Gellius is thin. Why shouldn't he be? He has a mother who is
so vivacious and who's a health nut
and such a lovely sister from the same bloodline,
a good uncle (perhaps too good!)
plus the influence of all those bouncing girls.
Now tell me why shouldn't he be lean?
Well, if he touched nothing
except that which was *unlawful* to touch,
you'd still find many reasons why he's so thin. (got it?)

98. Ad Victium

Victius, you filthy pig, you deserve to be called a loudmouth
because you won't shut up and besides you're such an idiot.
That tongue of yours never stops spewing a load of garbage
wherever you go, but guess what! you might be lucky one day
and get to lick a guy's anus clean and polish his Doc Martins.
But in the meantime, if you want to kill us all, Victius, just yawn:
The odor that comes out of your mouth will knock us out.

104. Ad Lesbiam

Could I even think to curse this girl I'm in love with,
who is the whole world to me,
who is even dearer to me than both my eyes?
Even if I could, I wouldn't, I can't,
I'm so desperately in love with her.
But *you* spend all your time with Tappo,
and commit every atrocity against me
with your kind and delicate touch.

52: Always Make It New

Is death the answer, Catullus?
Is that what you think?
Nonius, that puss-filled wart,
sits his fat ass in the consul's chair.
He's a lying snake and he says Vatinius agrees
that he has the right to the consulship.
Is death the answer, Catullus?
Is that what you think?

56. The Best Gag Around

Wow! a funny thing happened, Cato, what a riot!
You won't stop laughing when I tell you!
Laugh as much as you love your Catullus, Cato,
it's very funny and the best gag around.
I just caught a boy having sex with a girl.
And may it please Dione, I pulled out a grand boner
and speared him with it!

115: To The Cock

Mantula has something like thirty acres of meadow
and forty-fields: but the rest of it is marshland.
Why shouldn't he be able to exceed fat Croesus in riches,
who possesses so many assets, foreclosed houses, for example, as well as
meadows of hay, farmland, the vast woods and pastures and lakes
as far as the Hyperboreans, and the Ocean?
Sure all this is great, but Mantula's the greatest of all,
and I'm not speaking about the man, but about a great projecting Cock.

43. Ad Ameanam

Well hello there, Ameana, from the looks of it
I can see your nose is not quaint and your feet are ugly as hell!,
your eyes aren't dark and sexy, nor are your fingers long and elegant
your lips are not smooth and kissable,
your breath stinks, and you wag your tongue like a dog
when you speak!
I can't believe it! Is this Mamurra's girlfriend,
that fool of Formiae, who doesn't have a dime to his name,
is this the women known as the "the beauty of the provinces?"
What nonsense! Can she compare with my Lesbia?
I can't believe my eyes!
What decadent times these are.

32. Ad Ipsicillam

Ipsitilla, my sweetheart,
my sophisticated beauty, please, I beg you,
let me be your slave, let me stay with you this afternoon,
and, if you agree to have me, then please do me another big favor,
bolt the door so no client can interrupt us
just because he's had your ass once or twice before
and don't think of cruising the streets tonight,
stay home with me and prepare yourself
for nine – count 'em – nine quick fucks in a row.
But if you want it now, just say so, it's my pleasure to serve you:
I just finished a tasty lunch and my stomach's full
and I'm laying on my back
with my legs wide open
and my prick is poking through my tunic.

27. To His Servant Boy

Servant boy, take that old bottle of Falernian wine
and fill up my bitter chalice to the rim.
It's Mistress Postumia's Law!, the old whore,
whose always sloshed just like the drunken grape itself!
O Waters! go wherever you want and fill some other cup,
you're no friend of the Divine grape, go, instead, to those
uptight magistrates in their high towers
and pour them some Poland Spring!
This here is pure Bacchus, straight, no chaser!!!

24. Ad Iuventium

You, who are the youthful flower of the Juventius family,
sweetest of all, exceeding in riches all the other ones,
all who have ever been,
or will ever be in years to come,
I would rather you give all your shining gold coins
to that poor Midas over there
than allow yourself to be loved by that pig
standing under a statue with a bulge in his jeans.
You say "That one there? Isn't he hot?"
Yes, he is (I confess I have a boner under my tunic!).
But for all his good looks he doesn't have a pot to piss in!
Sure, you can bend over and let him fuck your tight little hole
all the while singing and laughing at me.
But it doesn't matter what you do,
that guy'll never be rich.
Don't you realize he doesn't have a penny to his name!

106. A Boy For Sale

When he sees an auctioneer with a beautiful boy,
what else can he think but that the boy is selling himself?

111. AD AUFILENAM

Aufilena, they say to live and sleep with one man all your life
"is the highest glory for a wife." Ok, maybe they're right.
You say keep it in the family! But then again, wouldn't you rather just bend over
and get fucked by one man after another? Wouldn't you prefer that
to giving birth to your cousins after fucking your uncle!

96. Ad Gaium Licinium Calvum

If anything pleases death, Calvus,
if the dead are grateful for anything,
it is for the bitter tears we weep for old friendships
and the renewal of old loves once torn apart,
and so the premature death of Quintilla, your wife,
should not be a source of despair for you,
your love brings her great joy even in death.

97: Ad Aemilium

No! (by Jove!) it made no difference whether I smelled Aemilius' mouth or ass,
as a matter of fact neither is more rotten and filthy than the other,
or rather the anus is the smarter of the two since it has got no teeth!
He instead has long wolf-like teeth, rotting gums like an old fart, and
in summer, his gaping mouth resembles a mule's vagina when she pisses.
He fucks many women, and makes himself out to be a charming man,
and yet why hasn't he passed his ass over to the baths
for a good working over in the "grinding mill"?
If any woman touches him, should she then have to
lick clean the ass of the executioner?
What sense does that make?

110. AD AUFILENAM

Aufilena, mistresses are always well off: they receive their price.
It's what they set out to do from the beginning.
But because you fucking lied, didn't give me a damn thing,
and because this happened more than once,
and because you promised me you were a virgin, I hate your guts.
Now every freewoman has a right to work in that whorehouse
just as every chaste woman has the right to refuse what they can't deliver,
             Aufillena:
but to receive gifts and then cheat me out of what I paid for
is more characteristic of a tight-fisted whore
who prostitutes herself with her entire body.

86. Ad Lesbiam

Everyone thinks Quintia is beautiful.
For me she's white-skinned, quite tall for a woman
and certainly well-built: I admit all of this is true. But "beautiful"
is not exactly the right word to describe her;
she's not graceful at all and her entire
white, tall, athletic body, isn't worth a single grain of sand.
Lesbia, on the other hand, is the epitome of beauty.
My bad luck is that it's her beauty
that attracts all these other women to her.

91. Ad Gellium

Don't think it's because we go back so many years
or I ever thought you weren't someone capable of fidelity, Gellius,
or that you couldn't restrain yourself from vile acts,
no, I really expected you to be true to me
in this miserable, ruinous situation that I foolishly call "love":
You knew that I loved *her*
and for God's sake it wasn't like she was your mother or your sister!
You knew this love was eating me up alive,
but you just went ahead and did it!
Just because we have been close friends, almost family,
this is no reason to say you want me, or to put your hand on my knee.
You're such a bore with your little transgressive games.
You enjoy making other people's lives miserable, don't you?

92. AD LESBIAM

Lesbia is always cruel to me
and she isn't silent about it either!
She may destroy me in the end.
Unless she loves me? Poor Catullus, where are the signs?
It's the same routine every time: You tell her what she's doing is wrong,
but of course in a very loving way! You can't win.
Poor Catullus, this woman will destroy you in the end.

59. AD RUFUM

Rufa of Bologna, the wife of Menenius, loves sucking Rufulus' cock,
you know her (right! that's the one), she's often seen wandering around in graveyards,
grabbing the cooked meat for dinner from the actual pyres of the dead
and running around like a crazed person
picking up the "baked loafs" that fall from the flames,
while the cremator with the goatee beats her over the head!

78. Ad Gallum

Gallus has two brothers, one of whom has the loveliest wife the other a charming son.
Gallus is good-looking, for he joins them all as lovers,
so that the beautiful girl goes to bed with the beautiful boy.
Gallus is stupid, and can't see that he has his own wife to deal with.
Instead, he instructs a nephew on how to seduce an uncle's wife.

41. Ad Ameanam

Ameana, that overworked cheap whore
just asked me for a full $10,000 for an hour with that fat ass of hers,
you know her, she's the one with that ugly snub nose
and she's Formiae's mistress, that guy who's flat broke and declared bankruptcy.

Get her relatives and friends together quick,
call a doctor, that girl's out of her fucking mind.
She'd better take another look in the mirror
and ask herself what she's really worth!

21. Ad Aurelium

Aurelius, you're the King of Vices,
not only of those in recent years
but of countless others in the past, (what you call your "glory days"),
and I'm sure you're cooking up still more surprises for the future!
Now I know you want to sodomize my boy.
You're not even subtle about it!
You begin joking with him, and soon your arm is around his neck.
You're a sly fox and you'd try anything to get a piece!
You even attempt to construct insane plots against me
but you don't stand a chance at defaming my reputation.
I'll shut you up with my cock.
You know if you'd only stop fucking with me I'd make peace with you
but now I'm pissed:
this boy will have to learn from you (remember your days as a street whore?)
what it is to hunger and thirst.
So back off, and put your meat back under your tunic for god's sake.
Don't push me or I'll rape your mouth with my cock.

100. Ad Marcum Caelium, A Thief

Caelius Aufilenus is with Qvintius Aufilenus,
brother runs after sister in heat, all flowers of Veronese youth!
What sweet brotherhood of love!
Which of these should I favor? I pick you! Your attentions aroused mine
and we formed a unique friendship
when the furious flame scorched my genitals.
May you be happy, Caelius, and successful in love!

73. Only Friend

Stop thinking so well of yourself and that you deserve anything from anyone.
Stop thinking anyone will return the favor.
Nobody appreciates anything, and everyone
bites the hand that feeds them. Treating anyone with kindness
is tiresome and you're even worse off if you succeed!
Sadly, no one depresses me more seriously and painfully
than he who I thought was a friend.

6. AD FLAVIUM

Flavius, you loud mouth, I know that if your mistress
was not a hideous wench, stupid and unrefined,
I wouldn't hear the end of it,
but I am sure, this time, that the girl you're fucking
is the kind men only fuck with the lights off ! and you're ashamed to admit it!
But while not a peep comes out of your mouth, the bed,
decorated with garlands and scented with Stygian perfume,
is evidence of a woman's touch and tells me you don't sleep alone,
just as the pillow worn on this side and that,
that side and this, equally! speaks volumes and, lastly, the shaking of the bed,
as it squeaks and bounces up and down, a thunderous noise!
But it's no use keeping quiet about your sexual escapades. Why?
Because you can hardly stand up when I'm speaking to you?
I suspect it's because you've given your thighs some workout!
Now, whatever you have to say, whether it's good or bad, you'd better speak up!
Because either way I'm going to shout what I know up to the skies
using all the power of my merry little poems!

85. Motto

I hate and love. Why do I do this, you ask.
>I don't know, but I feel it happening to me and it's torture.

72. Ad Lesbiam

Lesbia, you once said I was the only one for you
and that even Jupiter could not hold a candle to your Catullus.
I prized you above all others, not like any old lover, but like a friend,
and like a father who loves his son and his own children.
But now I'm wiser: and though I love you even more than I did then,
I think so much less of you now and your value for me has declined.
You say, "How can this be?" It's because the pain I suffer
causes me to love you more as a lover and less as a friend.

57. Ad Gaium Iulium Caesarem

These vulgar sodomites, Mamurra and Caesar, are the toast of the town!
No wonder! They're both equally contaminated, and from Formiae,
one is from the inner city, the other from the country
and these stains (the mark of depravity!)
are permanently imprinted onto their bodies like tattoos
and can't be rubbed off or washed out.
They're both equally advanced in the disease. They're like twins!
Both gained their education in a tiny bed,
both are masters of the "purple prose" i.e. dilettantes!
Neither is better than the other when it comes to adulterous blasphemies.
They're even rivals when it comes to fucking young girls!
So that's how it goes. People like Mamurra and Caesar
are considered the toast of the town!

69. Ad Rufum

Rufus, you wonder why no woman
is tender under the thigh, and why you can't get her to open her legs for you,
not even if you undermine her resistance with precious gifts
like a silk dress or fabulous jewels that glitter.
You're afraid the people are whispering that you're armpits stink
like the smell of a ferocious goat!
This woman is afraid of you and for good reason. Now tell me
what woman who would go to bed with a disgusting goat. (ok, ok,
but I won't mention her name in these verses!)
So either rid yourself of this horrible odor that repels her pretty nostrils
or stop complaining that every women you meet
won't give you the time of day but instead
runs right out the front door!

94. A Cock Is For Fucking

Cock adultery? An adulterous penis? Of course!
    As the saying goes : the pot always finds its own vegetables!

107. Ad Lesbiam

If you desire and hope for something and it arrives unexpectedly,
then your soul will be pleased. Therefore I am ecstatic,
that you, who are dearer to me than gold, you, have come back, my dear Lesbia,
and you want me again and I can't believe my wish was granted,
that you actually came back and are in my arms again.
My life falls on a brighter note!
Tell me what man alive is happier
and could hope for anything more than this.

78B.
(A Fragment)

….but now the reason I'm annoyed is that your filthy saliva
has polluted the pure lips of a pure girl.
(dear reader, I'll let you guess where his mouth has been!)
For this you'll be punished: for all the years to come they will know who and
what you are i.e. that your private passion is licking asses clean!

33. AD VIBENNIOS

Here in these excellent baths, the best place for fucking, I see
Vibennius the Father and his pansy son, both Thieves
(the father's got a lightning fast right hand to pick pockets with,
while his son sells his ass for anything he can get!),
Why don't you both go into exile, somewhere far off
since everyone here knows your whereabouts?
Your father's thieving is well known to the people.
And you, young man, couldn't earn a penny with that hairy ass of yours.

16. AD AURELIUM ET FURIUM

I'll bugger you and stuff your hole, Aurelius, and you too, Furius, you catamite,
since you both think my verses are rather prissy and indecent!
You say the true poet should be chaste in his life but not necessarily in his verses,
which have taste and charm if they are delicate and sexy
and can incite an itch in the groin, not only in young pretty boys,
but in those hairy old men who can't get their dicks hard.
So you read a line in one of my poems
like "I give you a thousand kisses," and you doubt my virility?
I'll show you fools what I'm made of.
I'll face-fuck you both and sodomize your asses till you bleed.

75. AD LESBIAM

Because I love you, Lesbia, and you always reject my advances
I suffer so much I fear that I'm going insane!
I couldn't love you even if you were the epitome of virtue
and yet I can't *stop* loving you
if you continue to do the worst imaginable things to me.

13. Ad Fabullus

You will dine well at my house, Fabullus,
if, in a few words, the gods favor you
that is, if you bring with you a good and tasty dinner,
and don't forget the pretty girls and wine, lots of it, and wit
and all kinds of loud laughter. Why these things you ask?
Well, my charming friend, it's because I'm broke
your Catullus' purse is full of cobwebs.
And yet, despite this, I have much love to give, or
something even better, more elegant:
I have a perfume, which all the Venuses and Cupids gave to my girl,
and when you smell it, you'll ask the gods to transform you, Fabullus,
into a big nose!

46. A Lyric

Now Spring brings back the warmth,
and the rage of the equinoctial sky
is hushed by the pleasant breezes of Zephyr.
You should leave the Phrygian fields, Catullus,
and the rich territory of scorching Nicaea: Already your thoughts
fly towards the famous cities of Asia.
Now the mind trembles with anticipation and yearns to leave
and the eager feet grow strong and begin walking.
Farewell, dear sweet friends and fellow travelers,
who having wandered far from home at the same time and who,
though travelling on different paths in different directions, have by a
single common route come together again.

103. Ad Silonem

Silo, if you read this, either give me back my ten thousand dollars, and then you can continue to be as violent and dominant as you like, but if the money pleases you and you'd rather keep it I beg you to stop being a pimp and acting violent and dominant at the same time.

81. Ad Iuventium

Juventius, from all the pretty men in all the bathhouses in Rome,
couldn't you have picked up
someone other than this young punk
from the filthy district of Pisaurum?
The only thing yellower than his complexion
is that old gilded statue of Caesar!
And, to make matters worse,
you say he turns you on!
You mean you like him more than me?
Can't you see you're being a real asshole?

83. Ad Lesbiam

Lesbia screams and insults me in front of her husband
and the simple-minded fool simply grins. He's evidently content
and knows nothing! Listen now, you mule!, if she could forget about me she'd shut up
and not throw these crazy fits: but because she whines like a little girl
and hurls curses at me, this means she remembers me, and what is
much worse, infinitely worse, is that when she's really pissed (like now!)
she works herself up into a state of rage beyond belief
and then begins to talk and talk and talk!

25. Ad Thallum

Thallus, you sodomite, your ass is softer than rabbit fur,
or goose marrow, or a tiny little earlobe,
or an old man's drooping penis, neglected and covered with cobwebs. And yet
when the full moon rises and you witness the guests beginning to nod and go to sleep,
your claws go to work like a furious hurricane. Give me back my fucking coat
which you pounced on and my fine Spanish table napkins and the painted boxwood
writing tablets which, foolish man, you kept on display like heirlooms.
Now unglue these items from your greedy claws and return them to me,
or I'll use a whip to print some really embarrassing lines,
as hot as the iron that brands disgrace onto the common thief,
on your soft as wool ass cheeks and tiny little hands.
It'll turn you on in a brand new and exciting way! Your head will spin in circles
like a small boat caught in a hurricane as the winds are howling like mad

40. AD RAVIDUM

You say it's a corrupt mind, poor Ravidus, that delves headfirst into my poems?
You invoke the gods for help? Believe me they won't favor you.
Are you looking for a fight?
Looking to get your portrait on the cover of Star magazine?
What do you want? Do you want fame at any price?
O you'll get it since you decided to fall for my woman.
You'll be on the first page of the Times: Catullus face-fucks Ravidus to death.

82. Ad Quintium

Quintius, if you wish Catullus to owe his eyes to you
or anything else, if there is anything else dearer,
do not snatch from him what is much more dear to him
than his eyes or what is much dearer to him than eyes.

112. Ad Nasonem

You're a whole lot of man, Naso, and yet many men dare ram their prick into your ass: Naso, you're one hell of a big guy and yet you take it from behind!

116. Ad Gellium

I've spent hours wracking my brain to find a way
to send you some poems of Callimachus,
that might soften you towards me, so you'd stop
trying to aim those bombs right at my head.
Yet I now see this labor has been in vain, Gellius,
and my good intentions have come to nothing.
But I'm older than you and your spears can't touch me,
you on the other hand, will be permanently fixed
like an arrow on a dartboard
until you give in!

90. Ad Gellium

Let a magician be born from Gellius' incestuous affair with his mother
and let him learn the Persian art of divination!
After all, it's important that a Magus be born when a mother fucks her son,
and, if that's the true sex magic of the Persians,
he should be grateful that he received the playlist to honor the gods with song,
as he melts horseshit with a torch on the altar!

49. Ad Marcum Tullium Ciceronem

You're one of the most eloquent orators
from the descendants of Romulus
and there are just as many others now,
Marcus Tullius,
and more to come!
But thank you for thinking of me,
the great Catullus
the worst poet,
the absolute worst,
just like you who are the Patron of all!
p.s. I wish you my best.

80. Ad Gellium

Gellius, what can I say is the reason
your rosy lips are whiter than snow,
when you wake up in the early morning around 8 o'clock
or when the afternoon sun gently rouses you from your siesta?
I'm not certain what it is:
whether all this whispering on the streets is true about you,
that you like to suck cock while down on your knees.
The people cry out that poor little Victor's balls exploded
and your lips have been stained with all the cum you couldn't rub off.

60. Cruel Heart

Did a lioness from the African mountains,
or Scylla barking deep inside your cunt,
or both give birth to a mind as rock hard as yours?
Why do you ignore the voice of the beggar
just like Scylla would have with her sadistic heart?

88. AD GELLIUM

What is my dear Gellius up to, lusting after his mother and sisters,
unable to sleep at night, tossing and turning, naked in his bed.
What does he do with his uncle, who he prevents from being husband to any wife?
Does anyone know the extent of his deviance and his guilt?
Is there really so much crime infecting this house?
It must be Gellis is such an extremist that not even Oceanus, father of the nymphs,
nor his wife Tethys, who lives at the very edge of the world, can wash away his sins!
It isn't possible for him to absolve himself of guilt, his crimes are legendary!
Not even if he bent down his head in shame and swallowed himself !

95B.

Let these small monuments of ...... please you (you know who you are!)
and let the vulgar throng rejoice in the pomposity of Antimachus

30. AD ALPHENUM

Alfemus, you're a Janus-faced punk and an uncouth beast
to all your friends who love you.
Don't you have any pity left, even a tiny bit, for me?
You've betrayed me and continue to deceive me,
you're tireless in your efforts to hurt me.
You know, these wicked deeds of treacherous men like yourself
are not pleasing to the gods.
The things you do to me are evil, you desert me and make me miserable.
And you don't seem to care one bit!
What is a man to do? Tell me, can men have faith in other men?
At any rate, you asked me to surrender to your will, no questions asked.
Can't you see how unfair that is! And me, Catullus!
Alfemus, you know you lured me into loving you,
made me think everything was all right, that I wouldn't be in danger.
And now you withdraw yourself again, your words, and all your deeds
are carried away on the rough winds and airy clouds and remain unfulfilled
You may have forgotten, but the gods remember everything!
Venus will make sure you're severely punished for these deeds in the future.

15. Ad Aurelium

To you, Aurelius, I entrust everything, even what I love most.
I simply ask, if you ever valued anything in your life
as pure and untouched, please preserve my boy-friend, Juventius,
from the vulgar throng - I don't fear them but I keep my mouth shut.
They roam the street, going here and there,
minding their own business. But then you never know!
But the truth is I fear your cock is hostile
to boys, both good and bad alike.
You let it go where it pleases,
as much as you wish, when you're travelling.
And when you're randy, I know you'll fuck anything!
But please keep away from my boyfriend.
I think I'm being reasonable about this.
But you must know that if in a frenzied rage
you start pushing me around,
thinking you're tough,
and your evil mind, intent on reaching your goal,
with its plotting and scheming, ends up oddly making me feel guilty,
then, I promise, you'll have a miserable and ill-fated life!
Why? Because in front of a huge crowd in the center of the city,
with your legs tied and your ass cheeks spread,
I'll stuff radishes and mullets right into your asshole!

87. Ad Lesbiam

No woman can truly be loved so much as my Lesbia was loved by me. No bond of trust in any other love was ever kept with such devotion.
At least on my part.

99. AD IUVENTIUM

I stole a kiss from you, honey-sweet Juventius, while you were playing.
Ah, it was sweeter than ambrosia!
But of course I paid for it.
It was like being nailed to a Cross for over an hour!
I tried to apologize to you, but my tears did nothing to appease your ferocity.
I tried but you wiped my tears from your lips in disgust
and washed them with plenty of water, wiping them with your fingers
as if my saliva was as filthy as a she-wolf's urine.
Love doesn't hold back from making me miserable.
I'm troubled and tormented in every way about this,
and for me that sweet ambrosia (now) tastes like the bitterest herb.
I am punished instead of this selfish lover!
When will you learn, Catullus?
It's not wise to steal a kiss from an idiot!

51. Ad Lesbiam

To me that man over there seems equal to a god
and I mean no offense to any sacred law,
but I think he even surpasses the gods.
He sits opposite you, repeatedly looks at you and listens,
I can hear your sweet laughter ringing in my ears,
and I am quickly silenced.
The result is my wretched state,
all my sense leaves me. Why?
Because I realize as he looks at you, Lesbia,
nothing remains for me.

* * * * * * *

My tongue is numb, a fire burns in my groin.
Now my ears are ringing with the sound
of their mutual laughter. I am insane with jealousy!
Thankfully, the night covers both my eyes in darkness.
Idleness, Catullus, that is your trouble,
the reason for your manic static and paralyzing despair.
Remember, a life of leisure has brought kings to their knees
and prosperous cities to utter ruin.

108. Ad Cominium

If it should happen, Cominius, that by the will of the people your life comes to an end,
in old gray age, withered and insane from leading a depraved life,
I, for one, have no doubt, that your tongue, enemy of all good people,
would be the first to go, sliced off and fed to the greedy vultures.
Next your eyes, that gloried in the sight of sin, would be scooped up like marbles
and devoured by a raven's black throat while dogs sucked on the trail of your intestines
and wolves chomped on all the rest of your now useless limbs!

105. The Muses Have Their Say

Mr. Cock strives to climb up Parnassus,
but the Muses (those sluts!) prick him with their pitchforks and yell, "GET OUT"!

Fragments

1.

I dedicate to you and consecrate this sacred grove, Priapus……..
in Lampsacus, where your house is and sacred grove
…….. Priapus……. especially for you,
who are worshiped at the mouth of the Hellespont, in the cities
and elsewhere.

2.

my passion is the MEAT

3.

you won't escape the bite of my poem

PETER VALENTE is the author of *A Boy Asleep Under the Sun: Versions of Sandro Penna* (Punctum Books, 2014), which was nominated for a Lambda award, *The Artaud Variations* (Spuyten Duyvil, 2014), *Let the Games Begin: Five Roman Writers* (Talisman House, 2015), two books of photography, *Blue* (Spuyten Duyvil) and *Street Level* (Spuyten Duyvil, 2016), two translations from the Italian, *Blackout* by Nanni Balestrini (Commune Editions, 2017) and *Whatever the Name* by Pierre Lepori (Spuyten Duyvil, 2017), *Two Novellas: Parthenogenesis & Plague in the Imperial City* (Spuyten Duyvil, 2017), a collaboration with Kevin Killian, *Ekstasis* (blazeVOX, 2017) and the chapbook, *Forge of Words a Forest* (Jensen Daniels, 1998). He is the co-translator of the chapbook, *Selected Late Letters of Antonin Artaud, 1945-1947* (Portable Press at Yo-Yo Labs, 2014), and has translated the work of Gérard de Nerval, Cesare Viviani, and Pier Paolo Pasolini, as well as numerous Ancient Greek and Latin authors. He is also presently at work on a book for Semiotext(e). In 2010, he turned to filmmaking and has completed 60 shorts to date, 24 of which were screened at Anthology Film Archives.

Made in the USA
Middletown, DE
12 August 2019